All Scripture references taken from the KJV of the Holy Bible, unless otherwise indicated.

**<u>Breaking My Mother's Curses;</u>**
***<u>Undoing the Unintentional Word Curses of My Mother</u>***

by Dr. Marlene Miles

Freshwater Press 2025

Freshwaterpress9@gmail.com

ISBN: 978-1-967860-84-5

Paperback Version

Copyright 2025, Dr. Marlene Miles. All rights reserved. No part of this book may be reproduced, distributed, or transmitted by any means or in any means including photocopying, recording or other electronic or mechanical methods without prior written permission of the publisher except in the case of brief publications or critical reviews.

## DEDICATION

To our mothers—
who gave what they could,
carried what they never healed,
and loved with the tools they had.
And to every child now walking in healing and truth—
may God restore what was broken
and bless what is yet to be built.

*Breaking My Mother's Curses –*
*Devotional Prayers for Healing*
*& Blessing*

## HOW TO USE THIS PRAYER BOOK

This prayer book is designed to walk you through a gentle journey of release, renewal, and restoration. It is not meant to be rushed. Let the Holy Spirit guide you at a pace that feels peaceful for your soul.

### 1. Come With an Open Heart

Find a quiet place. Breathe deeply. Invite God's presence.
You don't need the "right words."
You just need a willing heart.

### 2. Read Slowly, Not Quickly

These prayers are written to be absorbed, not skimmed.
Pause often. Sit with sentences that stir your heart.

## 3. Let God Highlight What You Need Most

Some sections will speak louder than others.
That is the Holy Spirit guiding your healing.
Follow His direction.

## 4. Use the Reflections Honestly

The reflections are not tests — they are invitations.
Let them help you uncover:

- what you inherited,
- what you believed,
- and what God now wants to heal.

## 5. Speak the Declarations Out Loud

There is power in spoken truth.
Even softly whispered, these

declarations reshape identity and renew your mind in Christ.

## 6. Repeat Sections as Needed

Healing is not linear.
You may revisit certain prayers many times — and that is holy.

## 7. Journal Your Journey

Write down anything God reveals:

- memories
- emotions
- breakthroughs
- new truths
- areas needing more prayer

This helps your healing "take root."

## 8. Do Not Rush Your Heart

There is no expiration date on healing.

Move gently.
Let God tend the places that hurt.

## 9. Invite God Into Your Family Line

These prayers are not just for you they are seeds for your children and generations after you.

## 10. Expect Transformation

As you move through this book, expect:

- clarity
- emotional release
- identity strengthening
- relationship healing
- and deeper peace

God honors every step of surrender.

## Table of Contents

**Opening the Heart Before God** ............................................. 11

**Prayer for Release from Hurtful Words** ................................... 13

**Repenting of Words I Have Spoken** ................................. 16

**Prayer to Break the Power of Negative Words** ..................... 19

**Healing My Identity** ............... 23

**Prayer for Freedom From Spiritual Influence** ................ 26

**My Relationship With My Mother** ................................. 29

**Releasing My Mother's Words** ............................................. 32

**Receiving God's Truth for My Life** ........................................ 35

**Declarations of God's Truth for My Life** ................................... 38

**Healing Emotional Residue** .. 40

**Blessing My Mother** .............. 43

**Blessing My Own Life and Destiny** ................................. 46

**Closing Sealing Prayer** .......... 49

**Closing Blessing** ................... 52

**WARFARE STYLE PRAYER POINTS** ................................. 55

Prayer Books by this Author ..... 74

# BREAKING MY MOTHER'S CURSES – DEVOTIONAL PRAYER MANUAL

*A gentle guide for healing, identity, and emotional restoration.*

**Opening the Heart Before God**

### Scripture

Let us therefore come boldly unto the throne of grace, that we may obtain mercy, and find grace to help in time of need.
**Hebrews 4:16**

Cast all your anxiety on Him because He cares for you.

1 **Peter 5:7**

### Opening Prayer

Heavenly Father,
Thank You for Your mercy, Your presence, and the gift of coming before You in prayer. Thank You for hearing me, loving me, and

covering my life with Your grace. In the Name of Jesus. Amen.

**Reflection**

**What do you need from God right now?**

_____

_____

_____

_____

_____

_____

_____

_____

**Declaration**

**I am fully seen, fully loved, and fully welcomed by God.**

# Prayer for Release from Hurtful Words

### Scripture

No weapon formed against you shall prosper, and every tongue that rises against you in judgment you shall condemn.
**Isaiah 54:17**

And to Jesus the mediator of the new covenant, and to the blood of sprinkling, that speaketh better things than that of Abel.
**Hebrews 12:24**

Lord, You see every word ever spoken over me.
Today I ask that every negative, harmful, limiting, or discouraging word—whether intentional or

careless—would lose its influence over my life and my children.

Your Word promises that every tongue that rises in judgment shall be condemned, and that this is the heritage of Your servants.
Father, let Your Truth rise above every harmful word.
Let Your voice be the loudest voice in my life.

Thank You that the Blood of Jesus speaks a better word—one of Mercy, protection, healing, and blessing. In the Name of Jesus. Amen.

**Reflection**

Think gently:
Is there a phrase that still echoes in your heart that God wants to quiet today?

**Declaration**

**God's truth defines me—not the words spoken in hurt or fear.**

**Repenting of Words I Have Spoken**

### Scripture

Set a guard over my mouth, Lord; keep watch over the door of my lips. **Psalm 141:3**

Death and life are in the power of the tongue. **Proverbs 18:21**

**Prayer**

Lord, forgive me for any words I have spoken that did not reflect Your heart.
If I have spoken hurtful or limiting words over anyone—including my children—please cleanse me and release them from the weight of those words.

**Lord, I withdraw every hurtful word I've spoken.
Cover them in the Blood of Jesus and restore what was damaged.**
In the Name of Jesus. Amen.

### Reflection

**Is there someone you need to release from your own words?
Let grace flow in both directions.**

**Declaration: My words will reflect God's love, wisdom, and truth.**

**Prayer to Break the Power of Negative Words**

## Scripture

There is therefore now no condemnation to those who are in Christ Jesus. **Romans 8:1**

You shall know the truth, and the truth shall make you free. **John 8:32**

**Prayer**

Father, in the peace of Your presence, I release every negative word spoken over me.
I lay them at Your feet and ask You to cancel their influence.
Where words have wounded, bring healing.
Where words have limited, open new paths.

Where words have discouraged,
speak hope.

I forgive every person who has ever spoken hurtful words about me, and I bless them with Your love and peace.

Today, I receive Your truth:
I am loved, chosen, and redeemed.
In the Name of Jesus. Amen.

---

**Reflection**

**Forgiveness is not about agreement;
it is about releasing the weight from *your* soul.**

## How has God shown you truth over lies?

_____

_____

_____

_____

_____

_____

_____

_____

_____

_____

## Declaration

**I am blessed, chosen, redeemed, and free.**

## Healing My Identity

### Scripture

I praise You because I am fearfully and wonderfully made.
**Psalm 139:14**

For we are His workmanship, created in Christ Jesus...
**Ephesians 2:10**

### Prayer for My Identity and Self-Belief

Father, help me overcome unbelief in any area.
Wash away every lie that makes me feel small, unworthy, or like a mistake.
Your Word says I am fearfully and wonderfully made.

Help me truly believe that deep within my soul.

Thank You that I am Your masterpiece—created on purpose and with purpose. In the Name of Jesus. Amen.

**Reflection**

**How would your life change if you fully believed God's opinion of you?**

_____

_____

_____

_____

_____

_____

_____

_____

_____

_____

_____

_____

_____

_____

_____

_____

_____

_____

**Declaration**

**I am fearfully and wonderfully made—crafted with intention and love.**

## Prayer for Freedom From Spiritual Influence

### Scripture

The Lord is my light and my salvation—whom shall I fear?
**Psalm 27:1**

Resist the devil, and he will flee from you. **James 4:7**

### Prayer

Lord Jesus, anything in the unseen realm that has tried to attach itself to the negative words spoken over my life—I ask You to remove it gently and completely.
Let every dark influence be

replaced with Your light, peace, and truth.

Fill my heart and my home with Your presence.
Let Your plans for me be unhindered and full of life. In the Name of Jesus. Amen.

**Reflection**

**What burden have you been carrying that isn't yours?
Let Jesus lift it.**

**Declaration**

**God's presence surrounds me; no darkness can hold me.**

# My Relationship With My Mother

### Scripture

Honor your father and your mother… **Exodus 20:12**

Be kind and compassionate to one another, forgiving each other… **Ephesians 4:32**

**Prayer for My Relationship with My Mother**

Lord, give me a heart full of love, honor, and compassion for my mother.
Where I have judged her, forgive me.
Where I have misunderstood her, give me grace.

Where there have been hurtful words, bring healing.

If I have ever contributed to her pain, please forgive me and cover her with Your comfort.

Restore her soul in every place it has been wounded.
Be her Shepherd and her peace.
In the Name of Jesus. Amen.

**Reflection**

Every mother is a woman with her own story.
Invite God to show you her through His eyes.

**Declaration**

**I honor my mother while walking in the freedom God gives me.**

# Releasing My Mother's Words

### Scripture

Love covers a multitude of sins.
**1 Peter 4:8**

Forgive, and you will be forgiven. **Luke 6:37**

### Prayer to Release Hurtful Words From My Mother

Lord, I forgive my mother for every hurtful word she has spoken.
I release her into Your mercy and care.
I choose blessing instead of bitterness.
I ask You to rewrite my story where her words shaped me in ways that were not Your will.

Father, help me gently let go of any words that said that I cannot live without her, I lack ability, wisdom, or common sense, I will not succeed, or I am limited or incapable.

I release those words now.
I choose to believe what You say about me. In Jesus' Name. Amen.

**Reflection**

**Which words do you feel God dissolving from your memory and emotions?**

_____

_____

_____

_____

_____

_____

**Declaration**

I release old words and receive God's healing.

# Receiving God's Truth for My Life

**Scripture**

> I can do all things through Christ who strengthens me.
> **Philippians 4:13**

The Lord will perfect that which concerns me. **Psalm 138:8**

**Prayer**

Father, I embrace Your truth about my future:
I can succeed.
I can flourish.
I can have healthy relationships.
I can build a stable home.
I can walk in confidence, beauty, and purpose.

Thank You for writing a new chapter of my life. In the Name of Jesus. Amen.

**Reflection**

**Where is God calling you to dream again?**

_____

_____

_____

_____

_____

_____

_____

_____

_____

_____

**Declaration**

**I can become everything God created me to be.**

## Declarations of God's Truth for My Life

Lord, thank You for speaking life over me.

With a peaceful and grateful heart, I receive these truths:

- I *can* succeed, because You strengthen me.
- I *will* become all You created me to be.
- I am capable of receiving nourishment, guidance, and support from You and from the community You provide.
- I can receive and keep a spouse according to Your perfect will.

- I can live, move, and have my being in Christ.
- I can build and maintain a home blessed by You.
- I can live with order, beauty, and balance without fear or bondage.
- My hair is my glory, as Your Word says.

Thank You, Lord, for making me whole. In the Name of Jesus. Amen.

## Healing Emotional Residue

### Scripture

He heals the brokenhearted and binds up their wounds. **Psalm 147:3**

Behold, I make all things new. **Revelation 21:5**

**Prayer**

Lord, wash away the emotional impact of words spoken during moments of frustration, exhaustion, or hurt.
Heal the echoes those moments left behind.
Fill the empty spaces with Your comfort. In Jesus' Name. Amen.

## Reflection

**Ask God to show you the difference between who you are and what was said about you.**

**What wound needs God's gentle touch today?**

___

___

___

___

___

___

___

___

___

___

**Declaration**

**My heart is being healed, restored, and renewed.**

## Blessing My Mother

### Scriptures

The Lord bless you and keep you; the Lord make His face shine upon you… **Numbers 6:24–26**

Live in peace with everyone. **Romans 12:18**

### Prayer

Father, I bless my mother in Jesus' name.
May You keep her, strengthen her, and give her deep peace.
Let Your face shine upon her.
Let Your love surround her.
May she know Your gentleness, joy, and rest.

Lord, I pray that You bless my mother and keep her.
Make Your face shine upon her and be gracious to her.
Give her deep peace—peace that protects her heart and mind.
Let her words and meditations bring You honor and joy.
May she flourish in Your love, today and always. In the Name of Jesus. Amen.

---

**Reflection**

**Blessing someone is an act of releasing control.
What do you need to hand over to God?**

**Declaration**

**I release my mother into God's hands and receive His peace.**

## Blessing My Own Life and Destiny

### Scripture

For I know the plans I have for you… **Jeremiah 29:11**

You will keep him in perfect peace whose mind is stayed on You. **Isaiah 26:3**

### Prayer

Lord, I receive Your shalom—Your wholeness, wellness, and peace.
Guide my steps.
Fill my journey with purpose, clarity, and strength. In the Name of Jesus. Amen.

## Reflection

## What new beginning is God inviting you to step into?

**Declaration**

**I walk in destiny, purpose, and peace.**

## Closing Sealing Prayer

### Scripture

The Lord will watch over your coming and going both now and forevermore.  **Psalm 121:8**

He who has begun a good work in you will complete it.
**Philippians 1:6**

**Prayer**

Father, I place all these prayers, reflections, and declarations in Your loving hands.
Seal them in my heart and in my future.
Let Your Spirit breathe life into every word. Surround me with Your presence and peace. In Jesus' Name, Amen.

**Reflection**

**Sit quietly and let God's Peace settle over you like a blanket.**

## Declaration

**I am fully seen, fully loved, and fully welcomed by God.**

## Closing Blessing

Father, I receive Your shalom—nothing missing, nothing broken—over my life and destiny.

Guide me forward with purpose. Fill my steps with peace, clarity, and strength.

Thank You for completing the healing You have begun.

In the Name of Jesus, Amen.

# WARFARE STYLE PRAYER POINTS

This section is for those who want stronger prayers in a warfare style. This is a near-exact transcript of the prayer points prayed at the end of the YouTube message of this same title.

1. Lord, have Mercy on me and thank you for the opportunity to come to You in prayer.

2. I speak no words of judgment or retaliation against anyone, but I do speak condemnation on condemning, judgmental, evil, wrong, limiting, biting, and hurting words spoken over me that are still in the atmosphere, that are still in the environment or hovering over my life. Any words still seeking after me, or my bloodline (my children) to cause opposition, hindrances, limitation, harm,

affliction, loss, or disaster, in the Name of Jesus. I condemn those words, in the Name of Jesus.

3. Lord, You said in your Word that we may condemn every evil word that rises up against us and I stand in that authority today, in the Name of Jesus.

4. No weapon that is formed against thee shall prosper; and every
tongue *that* shall rise against me, in judgment, I will condemn it.
This *is* the heritage of the servants of the LORD,

and their righteousness *is* of the Lord, saith the LORD.
Isaiah 54:17

5. Father, thank You that the blood of Jesus speaks a better word than any curse or careless speech. I renounce and denounce every negative word spoken over me (or my children).

6. Lord, forgive me, if I spoke condemning words or any words that amounted to curses over anyone, in the Name of Jesus.

7 Lord, I repent for every word I've spoken over my child that opposed Your will.
I withdraw those words and I place them under the blood of Jesus." I renounce ever having spoke those words, in the Name of Jesus.

8 Father, hear my repentance and remove any **agreement** with any destructive words that I've ever spoken over anyone, in the Name of Jesus.

9 I break the power of all evil words and I cancel the effect of all evil

words that have been spoken over me, in the Name of Jesus.
I forgive those who spoke evil words over me, and instead, I bless them.
I now receive Your truth, Lord: I am blessed, I am chosen, and I am redeemed.

10. I break every assignment of every demon, devil or unclean spirit that has been summoned to bring to pass any evil or negative words – or the effects of those words over my life, spoken by my mother or anyone in a mother's authority over

my life, in the Name of Jesus.

11
I speak life, I speak hope, and purpose into my lineage—into my own life and into my lineage, from this day forward, in the Name of Jesus.

12 I break every evil soul tie that binds me to pain, to limitation, to near success, to rise and fall, to darkness, to failure, to hindrances, to obstacles, in the Name of Jesus.

13 Lord, help my unbelief.

14 Lord removed any unbelief that keeps me

from believing Your Word completely. Any unbelief that keeps me from, believing Truth. Any word that keeps me from believing that I am fearfully and wonderfully made. Lord, break any unbelief that makes me believe I was or am a mistake, that I am lost, or cursed, or not good enough.

15 Thank you Lord that I am Your masterpiece, fearfully and wonderfully made. In the Name of Jesus.

16 Thank You, Lord that I am created on purpose

and with purpose, in the Name of Jesus.

17 Lord, give me respect and honor and love for my mother that is *agape*, approved, Godly and brings glory to You.

18 Lord, forgive me for any judgmental thoughts, words or deeds against my mother. Forgive me if I have ever cursed father or mother, in the Name of Jesus. Amen

19 Lord, remove that curse and wash me clean again by the washing of the water by the Word and by the precious Blood of

Jesus, in the Name of Jesus.

20 "Oh, that You would bless me indeed... and keep me from harm so that I will be free from pain." Change my name to the name You gave me if I have the wrong name – first name or last name, in the Name of Jesus.

21 Lord, in Your Word it says that *"God granted Jabez's request."* Bless me indeed, in the Name of Jesus.

22 "Lord, I forgive my mother for every hurtful word she spoke.

I release her into Your Mercy.
I choose blessing instead of bitterness."

23 "In the Name of Jesus Christ, I renounce every curse, label, and limiting word ever spoken over me by my mother (or anyone else).
I break all agreement with those words.
They no longer define me."

24 I love you, mom and appreciate everything you do and have done for me, but as hard as it may be. I must reject any words that you are spoken that

say, *I cannot live without you, or that any of us cannot live without you.*

25 I must reject words of limitation or words that say we lack understanding, knowledge or common sense, if the Lord says otherwise. I am on the Lord's side, and I believe what God says about me, it cannot be any other way, in the Name of Jesus.

26 I can be successful. I will be successful. I will make you proud, and I will be glory to God, in the Name of Jesus.

27 I can get nutrition without you; thank you for all you've taught me and given me. Now, I shine in the Lord, Amen.

28 I can get and keep a spouse as the LORD wills; the Lord puts the solitary in families, in the Name of Jesus.

29 I can live, move, breathe, and have being, in Christ Jesus Amen.

30 I can get and maintain a house. The blessings of the Lord make rich, and He adds no sorrow with it.

31 I can look neat and organized without creating idols.

32 My hair? It is my glory, according to the Word of God.

33 I am not judging you, I am weighing out these words that have carried over into my life that I am unconsciously obeying because you, as an authority figure spoke them over me, whether once or with repetition and regularity.

34 Lord, remove and wash away all words spoken when mom felt hurt,

unappreciated, unseen,
not cherished, in the
Name of Jesus.

35 Lord, forgive me of any
time I have ever been the
source of any hurt, pain,
sorrow, affliction, or
torment to my mother, in
the Name of Jesus.

36 Lord, be her shepherd and
restore her soul, in the
Name of Jesus.

37 Lord, I forgive my mother
for every hurtful word she
spoke.
I release her into Your
Mercy.
I choose blessing instead
of bitterness.

38 Mom, may the Lord bless and keep you, may He make His face to shine upon you, be gracious unto you. May He give you peace that passes all understanding. May the words of your mouth and the meditation of your heart bless the Lord always, in the Name of Jesus.

39 May the ***shalom*** of God be yours and may the shalom of God be mine as I pursue purpose and dash toward destiny, in the Name of Jesus.

40 I seal these words decrees, declarations and prayers across every dimension and timeline, past, present, and future, to infinity, in the Name of Jesus.

41 I seal them with the Blood of Jesus and the Holy Spirit of Promise.

42 Any retaliation against this author, the reader or anyone who prays these prayers, makes these decrees and declarations at any time, let that retaliation backfire on the head of the perpetrator to infinity, and without Mercy, in the Name of Jesus.

**AMEN.**

# Prayer Books by this Author

## Prayer Manuals

**FAKE FRIENDS:** *Prayers Against Betrayers*

HOLIDAY WARFARE Prayer Manual (humorous) Surviving Family Gatherings All Year Long (without catching a case)

SOUL TIE Prayer Manual (The) Part of a 3-part series including a workbook.

MAD at DADDY Prayer Manual – part of a 3-part series including a workbook.

Healing the Sibling & Relative Wound Prayer Manual

Healing the Father-Son Wound Prayer Manual

Prayers Against Barrenness: *For Success in Business and Life*

Breaking Curses of the Mother Prayer Manual

Prayers Against Barrenness: *For Success in Business and Life*

Fruit of the Womb: *Prayers Against Barrenness*

Beauty Curses, *Warfare Prayers Against* https://a.co/d/5Xlc20M

Courts of Marriage: Prayers for Marriage in the Courts of Heaven *(prayerbook)*
https://a.co/d/cNAdgAq

**Courtroom Warfare @ Midnight (prayerbook)**
https://a.co/d/5fc7Qdp

*About the Author*

*Dr. Marlene Miles* writes from a place of lived experience, personal healing, and a deep desire to see others whole. She knows what it feels like to carry painful words, to struggle with identity, and to long for God to rewrite the story. Through her journey, she discovered the power of prayer, reflection, and Scripture in transforming the heart.

Today, she shares those revelations with others—helping them break cycles, heal emotionally, and discover the beauty of God's truth over their lives. Her ministry flows with gentleness, honesty, and a prophetic sensitivity that reaches hearts right where they are.

Her calling is to help the broken become whole, the weary find rest, and the wounded step into purpose. Every book she writes is an offering of healing, hope, and freedom.

www.ingramcontent.com/pod-product-compliance
Lightning Source LLC
Chambersburg PA
CBHW060539080426
42453CB00028B/487